Talk is Cheap,

Until it costs you everything!

7 Strategies That Lead To Advanced Communication

According to Brian Tracy's, *Earn What You're Really Worth* (2012) the difference between people in the bottom 80 percent and people in the top 20 percent is simple. People in the top 20 percent have a different mind-set from those in the bottom 80 percent. Not only do the words that they use have different meanings, but their thinking styles differ as well.

Communication is more than words, it's a mindset, it's a skill contained in a package and the package is you!

By: **Avis P. Robinson, MA**

Library of Congress Cataloging in Publication Data

ISBN: 978-1-68419-069-0

For quantity purchases of this book contact:

OBE|Communication Consulting Agency

@

www.obecommunicationcoach.com

Printed in the United States of America

First Printing, 2016

Cover Photograph: © Tomas Anderson. Courtesy of 123rf.com

Contents

Dedication

I dedicate this book to the loving memory of my mother, the late Mary Lee Pettiford, for her years of sacrifice, which I never understood, and for lessons unseen and unlearned, until I had children of my own. To the memory of my father in the faith Clifford S. Davis for his relentless spiritual lessons, shared wisdom and knowledge of God, which has given me the spiritual confidence and courage to take this world by storm.

To my husband, Stephen Robinson for his long-suffering and constant free flowing love and patience. To my children, Syietta, Ryan and Kaylon for growing me up, their unconditional love, unyielding support, and for giving me eight grandchildren whom I adore. A very special THANK YOU to my church family, the Kivett Dr. Church of Christ, for their continued encouragement and never ending prayers that have helped me pursue my divine purpose.

There is no greater Acknowledgement, Dedication or Praise that I can give, than to my Creator. For, all that I do, and all that I am, is done in humble appreciation for the gifts entrusted to me. Thank you Father.

Preface

(By: Tanisha Harris, MA)

Eloquence and the ability to communicate effectively are often skills taken for granted and are drastically becoming a lost art. This is in part because we are seldom taught the difference between *talking* and *communicating*. We can all open our mouths and speak, but how many of us truly know how to align words in a manner that enables us to convey a clear message and that ultimately gets us what we want and or need? Knowing how to engage in effective communication enables you to advocate for your health, impress a potential boss, or diffuse an argument with your spouse, or simply cultivate a meaningful relationship, all of which can substantially impact your life.

Throughout my extensive research in health communication, I have heard many stories from youth about how they were afraid to talk with their partners, parents, and even their doctors about sex. Instead of asking the necessary questions to gain valuable, even life saving information to make wise and healthy choices, they remain silent, in ignorance and reap costly and sometimes deadly consequences. With the advent of the Internet, smart phones, and social media sites, we are constantly sending and receiving messages. Even though we have a multitude of channels to converse, our messages aren't any clearer. The proof has surfaced; simply talking more doesn't mean we have become better communicators.

After studying broadcast journalism at the University of Miami and receiving a Master's in Health Communication at High Point University, I considered myself to be a great communicator. However, it was not until I entered my doctoral program that I began to see more clearly how culture influences our ability or inability to accept alternate perspectives, or to be perceived in the light of who we are verses who someone may think we are. We all come to conversations with communication and contextual baggage. Being able to see the other side of the coin and understand the role culture plays in communication is a **key ingredient** to effective communication and what Robinson has brought to light, in a simple but meaningful way.

In this book, Robinson teaches and illustrates the difference between talking and effectively communicating with others and at its core is to answer "Why" it's this way. Unlike other books, Robinson emphasizes mental communication formation and the unique values and beliefs that influence our communication styles. She first focuses on how we need to change our way of thinking about talking so we can recognize our flaws, and then provides practical advice to equip readers with the knowledge needed to become better communicators over time.

The specialness about ***Talk is Cheap, Until it Costs You Everything!*** is how Robinson illustrates the communication breakdown in everyday life situations. She meets readers where they are. Instead of telling us what we should say or should have said, she challenges readers to analyze the often overlooked, minute details that cause common misinterpretations. It is through this reflection, we learn about the perspective of others, ourselves, and what it truly means to be a great communicator. No matter your profession or where you are in life, reading this book is well worth the read. It will help you become a better boss, employee, parent, spouse, patient, or professional. Whatever your particular communication need, Avis Robinson can guide you to becoming a more effective communicator that will be impactful to you and those you desire to communicate with.

Introduction

Objective research begins with no conclusions, but simply seeks out the truth. After more than two years of personal research, observation, listening to the stories of broken homes, battered relationships, lost jobs, offensive and misguided postings on social media and in social settings, it has lead me to know assuredly that there is a missing link in how people communicate. Communication style is a legacy that has been passed down from generation to generation. Therefore this book is a compilation of the past, present and future, as I have come to understand the observable barriers of communication. The outcomes of poor communication can be summed up as, broken relationships, increased crime, unrealized careers, stifled education, emotional dysfunction, and religious ambiguity.

According to Duck (1994), talk is the essence of a relationship. If this is true, it becomes almost impossible to communicate effectively if we don't know what the relationship is or what the talk is designed to achieve. Talk, for many, is grueling and uncomfortable; so, we engage only in surface conversation, we shut down, we blow up, cover up, shut up, and refuse to let anyone know who we really are, how we're really hurting, or we mistake pain for anger, which merely results in holding our true selves hostage.

Our internal stories become our reality; as they play over and over in our heads. Stories we have created to protect us from apathy, mistrust, disrespect, disconnection, and disillusionment (so we think). However, we behave based on the stories we believe. Culture absolutely affects how people communicate, understand and respond to the things around them. So, how can we make the changes in our communication and have the voice necessary to propel us forward? It begins with understanding "why" we communicate the way we do and finding the voice being suppressed beyond the words we speak. When your voices are truly heard, they will ripple across a nation which has never really heard your voice before. We can then speak peace into a new generation and for generations to come.

The genealogy of poor communication:

Uncontrolled emotions begat false perceptions and false perceptions begat distorted beliefs, distorted beliefs begat misshapen values, and misshapen values begat deficient communication, and deficient communication begat a circle of chaos and together miscommunication is conceived. On the pages to follow you will find seven communication strategies that will aid you in a practical understanding of communication and viable ways to facilitate your communication at an advanced and more effective level.

CHAPTER 1
Breaking Through Communication Barriers!

LTHOUGH, I DON'T KNOW YOUR PERSONAL communication stories, let's imagine together that your day unfolds a little something like this. For the sake of argument, let's say you're not a morning person, and you had an extremely long night.

The alarm doesn't sound and you and the kids wake late. Everyone is in a mass frenzy, one child hasn't budged at all and the other is moving at a brisk snail's pace; you're screaming "get up! get up! move it before you miss the bus! You've misplaced one of your favorite shoes that match your favorite top. "Arrgghhh, where is that shoe?"

The kids have finally kicked in to gear and are now clamoring for lunch money. You're screaming frantically at them to just get their book bags and homework before they miss the bus! They finally make their way out the door, and you belt out some other directives like "You better not lose that lunch money or else," and the door slams.

You drop to the couch, breathe a huge sigh of relief, as you think to yourself, "they" made it out alive. As for me, I'm only going to be thirty minutes late for work… that is, if I can catch all the lights on green. While in school, the kids are getting settled in to class, they're irritable and unable to focus; they just can't seem to concentrate. Running late means they missed breakfast; they're hungry *and* groggy. Nodding throughout the day, they just can't seem to pull it together.

Their teacher appears to have had a lack luster morning as well and she's unsympathetic to their lack of participation and delayed responses. To her this is becoming a more frequent occurrence. She tries to reach you with no response, so now she's even less patient with her student. To say your child's experiencing a difficult day is an understatement.

You arrive at work forty-five minutes late (not your projected thirty), and your day is unfolding in a similar fashion. You're much more abrupt today than usual. You too, are easily agitated. You call a staff meeting to talk about a deadline you are certain won't be met as planned.

The key project manager walks in prepared to explain the reason the project has been delayed, but you cut them off in mid-sentence, "you have more excuses than anyone I know! No more excuses, just solutions!" An imaginary line has just been drawn in the sand. They immediately shut down, instead of giving you all the critical information needed to continue to move the project forward. Now, both of you are in your feelings.

They are confident they have given the project 100%, and you simply refuse to acknowledge their efforts. Enthusiasm plummets, and you don't understand why. After all, that's clearly the way you see it. These can only be excuses, therefore, that's the way that it is. You're frustrated and so is the employee.

Days later, you really need guidance, the tension at work is much more than you care to take, you need this project complete and for now you need this employee. Getting guidance from work; not an option. You think to yourself, perhaps my Pastor can give me a word of encouragement after church services. What an insane week this has been. But this Sunday the Pastor seems distant, preoccupied, and rushed. He doesn't take the time to give you the attention you feel you deserve or need.

You leave feeling deflated and dejected instead of uplifted (which is what you had hoped for). You begin to question yourself, like, how dare he snub me that way? You know what? I've noticed he *never* really speaks to me. But, he *always* speaks to everyone else....And then you question his motives, what did I do to him? And you conclude with, he must not like me....

I know dear reader, you may never have felt this way, but I know many people who have. Yes, these may seem like either oversimplified or exaggerated scenarios, depending on your perspective, but these types of scenarios wreak havoc in lives each and every day, as we allow our perceptions in our personal, professional and spiritual encounters to run amuck. But, how did I arrive at this, from... "Let's say you're not a morning person..., you ask?"

These skewed perceptions are based on an inability to quickly cycle through amplified emotions; which in turn, cause our perceptions toward common every day events to be inaccurately assessed and magnified. The link between heightened emotions and assessment is often what proves to produce an impenetrable fortress. Processing of information in an overly emotional state is akin to the difference between objectivity and fantasy.

It is also this link that could create a faulty perception of your spiritual leader, which could lead to a waning faith and even dis-fellowship. It is this link which could cause an inappropriate assessment of an employee's efforts, resulting in disloyalty, discontent employees, as well as a toxic work environment. And it is this very same link which could cause our children (who are often times exposed to a barrage of screaming, and destructive criticism, without the balance of calm) to be poorly viewed, inappropriately assessed by teachers, faculty, and even their peers, as they mirror the communication they see and hear most often.

Dear reader, I am not speaking of isolated incidents. We all get overly emotional at times (yes, even me). I am speaking of consistent exposure to abrasive, mistrusting, berating, or demeaning behavior which creates diminished communication ability; which becomes as much a generational curse as poverty. Emotions are vital for day to day release, but unchecked emotions, breeds dysfunction. We are then forced to act or react from these personal frames of reference. A vicious cycle of emotionally driven communication then ensues, and unfortunately, we're in our feelings more often than we're out; an unstable place for decision making and accurate assessment.

However, when we think of passing things down from generation to generation, it is common to associate physical or tangible objects, such as a home, or inheritance. It is common to compare our physical attributes; and say things like, you look like your mom or your dad. You smile like your aunt, or you remind me so much of my sister.

This is particularly true of one of my granddaughters. Although, my sister passed away well before she was born, when I see her, I'm often taken back at how much her physical presence reminds me of my sister. So often, I have to catch myself to keep from sounding like a broken record. She is eight and has no idea (no frame of reference) of what this really means. So, when I do tell her, I make it a point to follow up with "what a beautiful child I think she is." This enables her to make the correct assessment of my need to compare her with someone she has never met. I become responsible for giving her a *positive* frame of reference.

However, of all the comparisons that could be made, we rarely connect our communication skills to family lineage. Do you tend to communicate more like your mom or your dad; your favorite aunt or uncle; your favorite teacher or mentor? The reality is we pick up habits, mannerisms, and traditional colloquialisms or sayings, from our circle of influence. Therefore, our communication ability tends to mirror the people who have influenced us most and at the earliest point in our lives, be that influence positive or negative.

One of my favorite musicals of all time is *My Fair Lady,* a 1964 Broadway musical film. I know, I just dated myself, but if you aren't familiar with this classic, please give it a quick internet search, and follow my train of thought. In the movie, Professor Henry Higgins, a phoneticist claims he can identify anyone's origin (where they were born) simply by hearing them speak. On a rainy night in London he runs into a shabby common flower girl, Eliza Doolittle, who has a dreadful accent. He makes the boastful claim that within six months he could provide her with speech lessons that would allow her to pass as a lady of distinction.

Professor Higgins also theorizes that proper speech (articulation) is what truly separates the social classes rather than looks or money, and under his tutorship Eliza Doolittle would be unrecognizable. This is no small feat to alter someone's learned speech behavior. The next day Eliza shows up on his doorstep to take him up on his proposition. However, should he fail she would be forced to compensate him for the lessons she'd received.

I have watched this movie more times than I can count on both hands. Not because of Professor Higgins phonetic ability, but because I love a good love story...and watching Eliza Doolittle transform into a fair lady, his fair lady, puts a lump in my throat every time.

But, today as a communication strategist, I now appreciate this movie even more. I watch the transformation unfold in a very different way. Sometimes, I even critique the story without the words and watch the body language to see if the meaning remains the same. For, Eliza not only transforms her speech, but her behavior is elevated. Finding a new meaning never really works because I've seen it so many times I already know what they're going to say. My perception is tainted, so to speak, so I see the same thing, I've always seen; a love story.

But in my called profession, I am forced to ask similar cultural communication questions, seeking to unravel my clients' true communication identity for the sake of their impending relationship, or to advance their stalled careers. Questions designed to reveal to the client, while answering for me as a coach, in order to enact positive change.

Was there peace and calm or conflict and contention? Do you have the ability to turn tragedy into comedy; and laugh until you cry or did crying suffocate the laughter? Or perhaps you come from a family of story tellers. Not liars, I mean actual story tellers. You know those orators who would sit down and tell you what happened in times past?

Ok, well, maybe they embellished a little.

You know that story about how they walked five miles to school in the snow with a hole in each shoe, without socks and a hand-woven sweater, no hat or gloves, and by the time they got there, they had frostbite on both hands and ears, and had to thaw out in front of a log fire before class began, and oh, they took all their notes with no pencil on a half a sheet of paper.

You know- that family. And did you do what I used to do? Look up at your mom with eyes of wonderment while in the back of your mind you're saying, really mom? Only half a sheet of paper! I literally, laugh out loud. It is a certainty; our communication is deeply engrained in our culture.

There's also a flip side to this communication coin. It's not always the way things are communicated to you, but sometimes the mere absence of what should be communicated, that never is. The "I love you's or "you're good enough." The voice of a man you respect who protects you and keeps you safe. A smile or wink that's offered when you make a mistake, and a gentle touch that signals, no worries, it's ok. As a product of a single parent home, this became painfully apparent to me as I sought out my own intimate relationships.

The way I communicated or failed to communicate with my husband was extremely difficult and emotional; a direct correlation to my base communication experience which resonated deep on a subconscious level. I simply did and said what I knew to do and say without giving it a second thought; my good ole frame of reference. It wasn't about the outcome or the good of the relationship. I cared little for how I was perceived, because honestly, I didn't connect communication to perception. After all, image management is reserved only for the elite, right?

So, what you see is what you get, and change could only result in me coming across as "fake." So, I was often told. And, I refused to be "fake", even if it cost me my relationship. I believe the phrase today is "Keeping it one hundred (100)." Well, I was well advanced in age when I began purposefully shifting my communication style, no matter what people said. I had finally come to the realization that changing how I communicated did not equate to being fake, but being better; and better was allowed.

We are all creatures of habit, especially in the way we handle our most intimate relationships. Our communication style--habitual; our approach to certain stimuli—habitual; and without an earnest desire to become better communicators, our ability to improve will remain unchanged.

Why, you ask, because change can only occur on a conscious level and all of the aforementioned habits occur subconsciously. Without putting in the work of change we will continue the cycle of poor behavior (no matter what the behavior might be).

Otherwise, we will remain in need of a communication transformation. It is only by advancing our communication skills that we become true cycle breakers. It is as urgent as seeking to live a healthy lifestyle. As critical as getting our blood sugar levels under control, in a nation plagued by obesity. It requires knowledge and guidance in much the same way.

Without it our relationships remain sick and failing because we have not connected the need to shift the way we communicate in order to save the relationship. This is not about accent or phonics, as was Professor Higgins' quest or the theory he proposed. It is about a meeting of the minds which there appears to be much less of. For the informed, it's transformational. For the uninformed it's life threatening, because what you don't know can surely kill you. Just ask anyone who's ever experienced a heart attack.

The single biggest problem in communication is the illusion that it has taken place.

George Bernard Shaw

Having taught hundreds of classes, the responses given by my students to the question "What is communication?" remains pretty consistent: talking, conveying a message, trying to understand, to be understood, getting your point across, verbal cues, body language...to date I believe I have reached saturation. I will however, continue to ask, just in case I'm pleasantly surprised. But for now, I have confirmation of just how difficult it is to pin down the definition of communication to just one thing. ***Communication Strategy # 1*: Redefine it.** Communication remains one of the hardest skills, to not only acquire, but also to define; because it's *everything* we do! Whether you like it or not, or think so or not, you are always communicating something, even in the absence of words.

Talking is merely a medium or method of communication. No different than texting a message, making a call, speaking into a microphone, writing a letter, reading a newspaper, watching T.V., or surfing the internet, they're all means of conveying and receiving messages, but not the message itself. Speaking louder, faster, harsher, or "having the gift of gab", being able to string a lot of words together, or the ability to articulate a sentence grammatically correct, does not make one an *effective* communicator. Knowing this truth is transformational.

The way you *define* a thing, is the way you *believe* it, and it is also the way you *live* it. To this point, if you define communication as "talking", then once you have spoken your message you might be inclined to feel that you have "effectively communicated."

However, more often than not, this is not the case. So, we speak thinking that we've done our part, while the receiver may still be in the dark. This incomplete definition, this insufficient understanding gives the sender a false sense of security and lightens their burden of responsibility; while it places a harsher burden on the receiver. This in turn translates into a lack of empathy and impatience if the receiver misses the message intended.

Then, what is ***Communication? (Robinson's definition)***: It is a behavior filtered through one's beliefs and values; a definition which I believe helps to identify what people are actually trying to say and do throughout the <u>entire</u> communication process (See fig. 1). What is the behavior you might ask? The behavior is *everything.* It's what you say, and why you say it. It's your nonverbal language, it's your posture; it's

your brand!

It's your silence, it's your micro expressions, it's a touch, it's

how close you stand in my space, it's your attitude, it's what you're

wearing, it's when you said it, it's how you said it (slow or fast, harsh or

soft). It's the perfume you wear, it's your hair. So much so, that singer,

song writer, India Arie had to write a song titled "*I Am Not My Hair*"

because we absolutely consider our fashion as an expression of what we

are trying to communicate, or how well we are being perceived.

Communication my friend, is EVERYTHING!

Fig.1

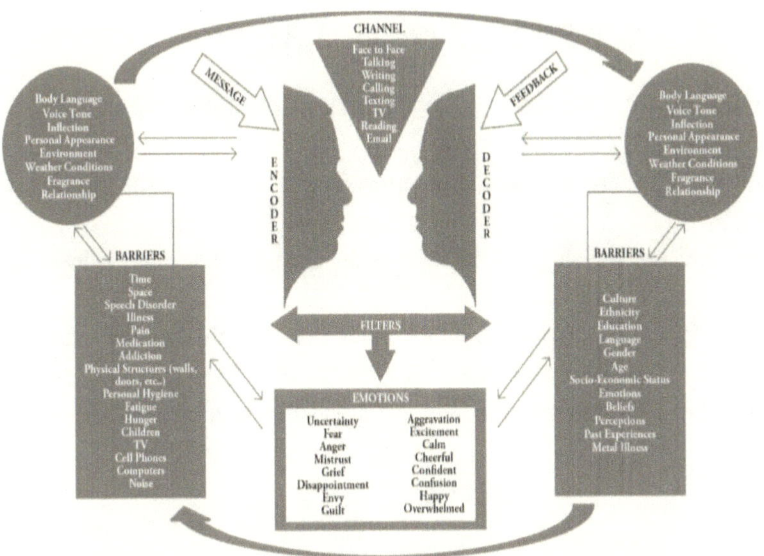

It is bound and inextricably tied to what we believe and value. It is a concept that has been grievously understated when defining communication and the communication process.

I vividly recall the day of my epiphany. The day that I realized that my husband and I were both speaking English, but two very different languages simultaneously. I said "you're wrong" and he heard "you're stupid!" He often uses this particular phrase in his communication style "You're trying to play me for stupid." I had heard him say it a thousand times if I had heard him say it once.

This day, I had challenged his beliefs about some subject, as I often do (unintentionally) and he said "You're trying to play me for stupid!" I said, "No, honey, I'm not." "You can be wrong and not be stupid." "You are one of the smartest men I know." "And these two things are not the same." Our discussion changed that day (at least for me). This was the revelation which made me cognitively aware that our concept of communication was skewed and had been skewed all of our lives.

We were doing it all wrong; simply because we didn't fully understand what it was. There was a vast difference in what I said and what he heard. That day my conversation would forever be changed. Not only would I become consciously aware of what I said, I would become equally aware of what I heard!

Just as we have a historical past so does our ability to communicate. The communication cycle within our relationships is often hindered by many historical barriers rarely ever mentioned, considered or revealed. And because such barriers have yet to be exposed we feel inadequate, we quarrel and fight, we curse and swear, we walk out, and strike out, we break dishes and slam doors, we sleep on the couch, we miss meals, we lie and we don't know why.

We call it irreconcilable differences and we use scare tactics and make threats. Without the ability to put our finger on just what happened during the message transmission that has caused us to be derailed, we place blame and defend ourselves against an unseen force. In turn, this forces us to point fingers and keep score. After all, I know you heard me clearly (so it seemed)? You acknowledged what was said, right? You nodded your head in agreement, right? We agreed that we were on the same page, right? Then what in the ham sandwich happened from then to getting it done? So, whose fault is it? It has to be on the part of the receiver, 'cause it certainly ain't mine! I was very clear, no miscommunication here!

But, not all barriers are created equal. Some cannot be corrected, but many can, *if* you know what they are and you're willing to take the time to enact change. These unidentified barriers result in bruised feelings, they cause us to disconnect ourselves from our relationships; whether physically or mentally. We become frustrated and agitated and we have very low tolerance for people who don't get us. These barriers cause us to over inflate emotions (Greene, 1998) and under estimate intentions, they're powerful, and they tug at us and give us great angst.

They cause us to avoid those critical conversations, or we have them, and say the wrong things the wrong way or the right things at the wrong time. We engage in sarcasm and snide remarks like "I'm just not feeling it, or them," "They're so stupid", or "I don't get it" "Why can't "they" get it", or "what else do I have to say for you to get it?" And the saddest commentary of them all, after many failed attempts we simply give up, or concede to be miserable. We throw our hands up in defeat and we walk away, and neither the sender nor the receiver realizes what really has transpired behind the barricade of barriers.

The relationship, ruined, and again, who's to blame? In order for this communication failure to make sense to us we gotta' blame somebody. Otherwise our communication is abstract and not concrete and we're groping in darkness. Unfortunately, if and when, the relationship ends, neither the sender nor the receiver, have gained any insight into themselves or how to prevent it the next time. So, we take our flawed communication style into the next relationship, into the next job, the next social setting and the cycle begins again.

But, if we're concerned enough about what has taken place, if the relationship really meant anything, and if we want to become better at this communication thing, we will seek help, and make a personal investment, perhaps in counseling, a book or a workshop which enumerates the skills needed to be a more effective communicator. And although, you try these things, the barriers remain a mystery. Without addressing the *why*; we are forced to return to a vicious cycle of the blame game, without truly becoming better communicators. The process of communication is going to require a shift in thought in order to move you to the next level.

So, please allow me to shed some light on just a few of the communication barriers we are forced to contend with day in and day out, communication encounter after communication encounter. Below is a small list I consider the most common and detrimental barriers to the communication process (fig. 2).

Fig. 2

Physiological Barriers	**Psychological Barriers**
Time	Culture
Space	Ethnicity
Walls	Age
Doors	Gender
Illness	Education
Sleep Deprivation	Language
Medication	Authoritative Status
Addiction	Socio-Economic Status
Hunger	Emotions
T.V. / Computer	Beliefs
Cell Phone	Perceptions
Children	Past Experiences
Noise	Mental Illness

Note: This in no way is intended to be an exhaustive list.

These barriers could exist at any given time within any sender or receiver of the message. Therefore, a person who seeks to be an effective communicator should give consideration to any possible barrier and seek to address it whenever possible. Take a step back and ask yourself, what could I be missing?

Patience and perspective while trying to communicate is critical; just because "that's how you see it", does not mean that's the way it is, or the way it's being received. Unfortunately, what usually happens is the person who sends the message gets angry at the receiver if it results in miscommunication, when in reality it's *your* message. How bad do you want me to get it? How important is it that I get it? Then we must be willing to go the distance. Patiently, go the distance. Communication becomes fruitful/productive if and only if the message sent by the sender is interpreted with the same meaning as the sender intended. It is your responsibility as the sender to convey the message in just such a way; and that may take time.

Below is a brief story and an example of my own personal experience where I have identified and inserted the possible communication barriers in ( ) for the sake of emphasis. (These are my own physical and psychological barriers).

I can recall as an adult learner/nontraditional student (age) how poor communication (perception) played out often between me and my peers (age, culture, gender), as well as my professors (age, culture, gender). I'd been out of school for some 20+ years (time, culture); with a family, a husband, and full time job (work, culture), and what I call "normal life crisis" (perceptions, beliefs). What higher education means for me, is that the information provided has a much richer context (beliefs, perceptions) since I have many more experiences to draw from (perceptions, past experience) or either it totally lacked context, if I thought it was too far beyond my years (my beliefs, whether true or not is irrelevant). Attending school in the evening (time) after a full day of work (tired, sleepy, hungry), meant on most days I had already reached information saturation (noise). I felt (emotions) my peers and even professors often saw me as "too deep, un-relatable" (perceptions, beliefs), because I asked too many questions. I wanted greater clarity and more information than the average student seemed to care for (education, emotions, beliefs). Having been told by my mother many years passed (time, culture) "Once you get it, they can't take it back (one of those traditional colloquialisms that meant knowledge is yours to keep, get all you can). So, what was perceived as un-relatable by many (perceptions) was me simply getting everything made available to me. Admittedly, I struggled in many areas (authoritative status, socio-economic status, beliefs and perceptions) to understand where the professor and the privileged students (perceptions) were coming from; having struggled financially all my life (emotions, socio-economic status). But the gain at the end was much greater than the immediate discomfort I felt (perceptions, emotions). I began to unravel the lessons learned, and peeled back the onion of communication in a much more profound way than it was being taught (beliefs, perceptions) so I thought. This insight has lead me down a path that I believe will help the average person who doesn't understand why communicating is so difficult, personally, professionally and even spiritually.

This story takes us back to my definition of communication: a behavior filtered through my beliefs and values. The way I communicate with you, and you with me, is based on what "we" believe (true or false) and value, and the barriers, are most often overlooked. I feel confident if my peers and professor were to share this story it would read quite different.

The outer conditions of a person's life will always reflect their inner beliefs.

James Allen.

Making the communication shift:

- Redefine communication to encompass everything you do instead of just the method used.
- Consider the possible barriers if you're not getting through.
- Resist the need to place personal blame and keep score.
- If at first you don't succeed, try, try again and again.

As a side note dear reader, I titled the first chapter "Breaking Through the Communication Barriers" because so often we try with all our might to break down our walls, to no avail, but perhaps if we could simply "breakthrough" and catch a glimpse of light, it would keep us motivated on to victory. Breaking down barriers is hard, but not impossible, but a breakthrough is a breakthrough no matter how small the hole. Just keep breaking through and eventually we will make it to the other side.

CHAPTER 2
I Can See Clearly Now

Singer, JOHNNY NASH RECORDED, *I Can See Clearly Now the Rain is Gone* (1974)….and all of the bad feelings have disappeared (I know, you might not know the song, take a second and give it a search). There is something very telling about being able to see clearly and having all the bad feelings disappear, which brings us to our next communication problem, which we all seem to face more often than not. ***Communication Strategy # 2*: Minimize Ambiguity.** Our brains hate ambiguity. But, what is ambiguity, so we can fully understand why our brains hate it so much?

Ambiguity is defined as: uncertainty, vagueness, doubtfulness. No wonder we hate it, we all want to be clear and especially certain about everything, right? So, wherever there is an unanswered question for us, what do we do? We answer it. We fill in the blanks! What's unfortunate about our need, and our ability to do this, is very rarely are the blanks filled in with positive information. Sad but true.

Let's take a look at a relatable scenario…Have you ever been waiting for someone to show up for a specific reason and they're running late? Minutes tick by and no call…you wonder, why are they delayed? They said they were on their way, and that was an hour ago. Since you haven't heard from them your mind needs an immediate answer, to your pressing question. You need closure, yes, closure and it has nothing to do with being a female. You need to determine in your mind the reason for the tardiness. So, your mind does what it does best, it begins to answer the question with the least amount of information; with what you feel is the most likely cause. It creates a story to the unanswered question. Why is the person late?

But far too often we come up with the most God-awful scenarios based on our previous *experiences* and *belief* system (even if our belief systems are flawed). We begin to reason, perhaps they were in a car accident (our autoimmune system gets ramped up) we get anxious, and we could even begin to worry, our hearts may race and our blood pressure may rise. Well, we didn't see anything on the news, or we didn't hear a siren, or get a call. So, what if they were stopped by the cops, or what if... they're cheating! And on and on and on our minds, will go.

The later the person is, the more time we have to think, the more details we add to the story. So, by the time the person has arrived we are either deeply distraught, filled with worry about their safety, or so mad we could spit bullets (depending on the type of relationship you have of course). The key is not to focus on the type of relationship in this scenario, but to develop the habit of positive thinking! Stop your negative story in its tracks. You can, you know- change the story, but only if you want to. You just have to want to. Give the person the benefit of the doubt or simply the benefit of some positive thought!

Create for them the story you would want told about you if you were late. Simple enough right, but extremely difficult if your historical, habitual, or pathological thinking and past experiences have made you cynical, mistrustful, doubtful, and fearful of being hurt. Your need to stop the hurting, accusing, and mistrust, or simply getting it wrong has got to be greater than what you're currently experiencing for you to make the shift. Hey, I know that you're tired of ineffective results, or you wouldn't have picked up this book. You want the help, you want the answers, but, what I have identified in my own life and in the lives of others, is how desperately we want to change, but aren't really sure how.

On the flip side of the coin of creating stories from past experiences, what if you are the person who arrived late? And you are also the person who isn't big on details, woe unto you. Now you're tasked with making your story refute or match the stories I've been creating.... filling in my blanks with whatever I can dream up. Many of us either don't say what we mean clearly enough, or what we say isn't received in the manner which we intended; this is the culprit which has created this historical cycle of ambiguity.

We hate the *feeling* of being misunderstood; that sinking feeling of having said all the things we thought to be important, and having them dismissed. We hate the arguments that could have been prevented; should have been prevented. We hate being cut off in mid-sentence and accused and being labeled a liar.

We hate that our reasons are twisted and defined as mere excuses. We get all "in our feelings", and struggle to say just enough, for fear of saying way too much; which in turn gives the receiver more ammunition to use against us, and hang us with our own words. S*o,* instead we have been conditioned to *withhold* them.

However, they demand more and more information; corroborate your story! At which time we become both judge and jury. Then our historical and habitual instinct goes into overdrive, we become more aggressive, and they become defensive. We scream, we shout, after all, we have to just get it out! Whoa! Stop! This all started because of *lack* of details; and the funny thing (not really) is, we fail to realize that no one

can tell you *every detail* to a story. We are trained to chunk information

by category or value. So, what we normally share is what we feel are the

most important details first.   When pressed, we search our minds for

more information to satisfy the person on the attack.

If you have ever watched one of those criminal cases on T.V.,

you have seen this approach during a police interrogation. The cops are

relentless in asking question after question, listening ever so carefully as

suspects reveal more and more details. They are waiting for one detail to

disprove another. Before you know it, the suspect is in too deep, and

shortly after being tripped up with one detail too many, they've

confessed; and sometimes, even to a crime they didn't commit.

In the *"Unlimited Power"* by Tony Robbins, he states that "the

words we use to describe our experiences aren't the experiences

themselves; they're just the best verbal representation we can come up

with (p. 276)." So, it's not that the original story wasn't true; perhaps it is simply our lack of ability to use the best words to describe our experiences; perhaps.

I know, you may be saying "sure, that all sounds good, but what about when they're lying and I know they're lying?" Yes, there are times when we flat out lie by omission or commission! But there are also times (more often than not) when we share what we feel to be pertinent without the intent to deceive. There are also those times when we withhold information because we are flat out insulted by unfounded accusations and constant interrogation.

Again, because we don't want to be misunderstood, we think less is more. So, we give as little information as possible, while the receiver continues to fill in the blanks. If you start out letting me make up my own story don't expect it to be pretty or positive. Please, don't give someone else that level of control.

There is always chatter going on inside our heads while the other party is speaking (that's internal noise). We're often asking and answering our own questions. We're surmising and speculating what's true and what's a lie. Some of us feel we are human lie detectors and we accuse with pin point precision. When the accused finally gets the chance to offer feedback or ask a question, if it's not what we wanted to hear, **our story**, becomes the **true story**. Lord, help us clear the confusion and quiet this inaudible noise.

Now, what we're arguing about *is no longer* based on the absolute facts of what has occurred, or not occurred. You're arguing, screaming and shouting and "mis-communicating" about what **you think** has occurred. When we deliberately leave a void it never leads down the path you want to go. I've learned this the hard way, more times than I care to count. Even if an argument doesn't ensue, the blanks are still being filled in with something; you choose.

Be open, be honest and by all means fill in your own blanks! Incomplete information is almost always filled with worst-case scenario stories. Let us do a better job of giving people honest stories of good intentions, right actions, and positive outcomes. After all, do we really want more information to digest and sort through? Or do we just want to believe the messenger. But, because our radars are constantly engaged in high alert, we want to control the hurt. We approach every encounter with suspicion. We must prevent pain at all cost (real or perceived). So, it just becomes easier to accuse, than to admit that I allowed you to make a fool of me.

By all means give information that will help to create the best outcome! And dear receiver, if you receive my story as true or even possible, please create the environment that truth is welcome, even if it seems unbelievable to you. For, if I feel my truth will be well received you are more likely to hear it, again and again.

Note to sender and receiver: There is danger in being in a relationship where someone feels betrayed, taken advantage of, or deceived; heightened emotions can lead down a slippery slope.

There is no greater impediment to the advancement of knowledge than the ambiguity of words.

Thomas Reid

Making the Communication Shift:

- Bring your thoughts under your subjection instead of letting them run amuck and ruin your communication.
- Skewed perceptions tend to amplify or diminish data, regardless of facts.
- Don't allow poor perceptions to reign supreme.

CHAPTER 3
You Just Gotta Get 'Outta Yo' Feelings!

THERE IS A TRUE DISTINCTION BETWEEN EMOTIONAL communication and objective communication, which brings us to *Communication Strategy #3:* **Be the Master of Your Emotions.** Being overly emotional is the downfall to decision making, and aggression stalls communication. You're less likely to make a mistake when you're not angry. Why, you ask? Extreme emotions can cause a temporary mental shutdown (Arden, 2010, pg. 65). The amygdala, the area of the brain which is referred to as the seat of where our emotions reside, once engaged, it can halt logical reasoning. According to Arden

(2010) "Once the amygdala gets excited, it doesn't care about context."

So, what you're upset about is not the circumstance itself, but simply

how you feel about the circumstance.

The knowledge which elevates our ability to effectively

communicate is in knowing that emotions are not dictated by *external*

circumstance. Meaning, that phrase we often use "You're going *make me*

go there!" is only true for those living in a reality controlled by someone

else. What takes you there, and what's creating this emotion is *you*, and

your perception of the circumstance you're in.

To gain emotional mastery, we must first exercise and engage

your logical region by the following acts: change the way you perceive

the situation, change the way you react to the situation, and then change

how you interpret the situation. Otherwise, your emotions will continue

to control you.

Here is a great opportunity to be reminded that communication

is more than words, it's a skill; a skill which enables the user to transcend ethnicity, gender, age, status, or title, and even excessive emotion. It has been often said "If you do the same old thing you've always done, you'll get the same old thing you've always gotten." Our emotions habitually follow the same pattern, only to produce the same results. First, there's a circumstance, then a thought, and then the feeling. Therefore, if we can change the thought, we can effectively alter the feeling.

If you are quick to anger it is a sign that this is the emotion you call upon most often. Many of us no longer get angry, we stay angry. "What do you mean stay angry?" Anger is at the ready. An inability to manage your anger causes an almost instantaneous flair up, supports that you are controlled by others more than you are able to control ourselves. Therefore, we must discover the root of what's making us angry or keeping us angry and expose it to the light in order to destroy it. Then, use the same light to point you in the right direction.

Sadly, we're using our anger as a high beam search light to point out every flaw we see in someone else. We have become cynical critics in the worst sense. What's eating us may be causing us to chip away at the self-esteem of those around us. It is lack of emotional control that leads to a pattern of verbal assaults. You're hurting and subconsciously your tone and word selection follow your feelings; and cut like a knife.

Failure to gain emotional control, or to become masters of our own internal universe, will force us to resign control to someone else, and allow them to jerk our emotional chain at will. This most often results in chaos and the worst possible outcome. After all, who wants to be on an emotional rollercoaster without having bought a ticket to ride? To possess a high level of emotional control prevents frequent bouts of anger and distress; while also easing your communication and how people receive you. If you are perceived as emotionally unstable and unpredictable, your communication is strained before it ever begins.

Great anger is more destructive than the sword.

Indian Proverb

Making the Communication Shift

- Take 100% responsibility and control of all your emotions.

- If you are emotionally distressed about a situation or circumstance it is due to your own estimate of how you see it. You can change it.

- This isn't easy. Our minds resist paradigm shifts-we don't like to change our fundamental perceptions of life.

- Once you master this, your life and the way you communicate will never be the same.

CHAPTER 4
Change Your Expectation or You're Gonna Miss it!

I N AN EPISODE OF THE HIT WESTERN *Larime*, aired on GRIT TV, "TV with backbone." You know the drill by now…please, give it a quick look up. Slim Sherman and Jess Harper, two good old cowboys who run a relay station out West, are often called to defend the peace in this new unchartered territory. In this episode, the bad guys have kidnapped a store keeper and are demanding that one of their gang members be released in exchange for her life, or she's surely gonna get it. Bite the bullet that is, take one in the back, or whatever they did to kill women in the old West.

Slim and Jess have been deputized and they are trying to figure out the best way to handle the bandit's demand, without releasing their prisoner and causing the damsel harm. Slim comes up with a brilliant idea. They will dress up another deputy in the clothes of the prisoner, set him on a horse and send him through the pass. Of course, he will be armed and Slim and Jess will be right behind him.

> **Jess:** Slim I'm not sure this is a good idea. They will know it's not Tom.
>
> **Slim:** No, Jess they won't. They'll see what they expect to see, nothing more and nothing less.

This was one of those moments I grabbed pen and paper, jotted down the quote and slowly nodded my head in total agreement for several minutes.

Yeap, we see what we expect to see, nothing more and nothing less.

Unfortunately, because of our inability to recognize subtle changes, we miss the small yet significant things that lead to big changes. Unless, we're looking for it, we're bound to miss it. Think about what you're thinking, the ideas you've formulated about a person and weigh these perceptions against reality. Particularly in our personal relationships we spend a great deal of time trying to turn our mates into mini Me's. We critique how our partners squeeze the toothpaste, whether they put the tissue on the roll facing front or back or whether to tuck the edges of the sheets or leave them loose, all based on *our* personal preferences.

If your partner begins to shift their way of behavior, to your way, they may have to point out the change initially for you to notice it. Or, if the change isn't drastic or consistent you may forget there was ever an attempt made to alter *their learned behavior*. Which brings us to *Communication Strategy # 4:* **Look for subtle changes and praise them.** Use the words "never" and "always" formed in a negative context will kill any spirit of change!

For example: "You *never* put the top back on the pickle jar!" You *always* leave the light on in the laundry room! This type of continual character assassination will lead you to communicating with the fictitious person you have conjured up by your false perceptions and not the person right in front of you. Because, even if your partner or child, put the top back on the pickle jar just once (in an attempt to change), *it negates never.*

The difference between communicating with the partner or child you have, and the partner or child you want them to be, is called an illusion. Being overly critical is crippling to any relationship; personal or professional. It's like pruning a tree too soon or too much, you stunt its growth if you cut too deep, and in many cases, it will wither away and die.

However, because we spend so much time chasing the illusion of the perfect person, instead of coping, appreciating, and requesting change with compassion, the relationship becomes gridlocked. We cycle through the same conversation over and over, resolving nothing. Resentment grows as the person that is constantly criticized feels more and more inadequate. "If I can't please you, why try." You're spinning your wheels and digging in way too deep. And since you're making no progress, frustration settles in for a long winter's nap, while hurt and rejection rattle around like the ghost of Christmas past. When this happens, laughter, affection and intimacy–simplicity and passion become dormant; and resurrection seems impossible.

Mature communication looks past flaws, understanding that there are no perfect people, and that an imperfect partner is all that an imperfect person like us can aspire to. By failing to communicate through failings and short comings we condemn ourselves to a life of loneliness; because imperfect people are the only kind that exists.

Making the communication shift:

- Alter your expectations, if you look for good you'll find it.
- Resist being overly critical, it stunts relationship growth.
- Refrain from using words like "never" and "always" unless used in positive context. "I will always love and respect you and I will never give up."

CHAPTER 5
Listen Up!

MISCOMMUNICATION IS ENTRENCHED IN THE SYSTEM of our beliefs. There is a most appropriate quote by *Steven Covey* which states "We see the world not as it is, but as we are, or as we have been conditioned to see it." ***Communication Strategy # 5:* Expand Your Perceptions Beyond Your Own**. We either assume that everyone sees the world in the exact same way or something must be terribly wrong with *them*! Another appropriate place to revisit my definition of communication: A behavior filtered through our beliefs and values.

We are desperately trying to connect with our spouse, a parent, a client, our boss, a wayward teen, a friend, a church member, and no matter what we try, it seems to be to no avail. We even try the things we know won't work. Shouting insults, bouts of silence, and still no results. We've hit a brick wall on more than one occasion, with more than one person. We're exhausted and powerless and so are the people we seek to communicate with. The relationship and the communication have reached an impasse. And herein lies the rub.

If talking is the essence of a relationship, then listening is the very essence of true and meaningful *communication*. To become a better communicator, we must *first* become a more empathetic listener. Let's be clear, not just any old listener, but an empathetic listener. At the end of the day, communication is not as much about teaching us to become better "talkers" but better listeners; the type of listener who is both physically and mentally quiet; the mother of all skills. The end result is to move us beyond our innate filter to be understood, rather than seeking first to understand (Covey, 2004).

Radical, right? Like, who cares if I understand you, isn't this all about me? Oh, contraire grasshopper! Your ability to listen exhibits a direct correlation to the value placed on the relationship of the sender. *I know, right?* Who knew? When we fail to listen to the sender we may be conveying (an unintended message, I hope) of devalue. I feel certain we care something about the person we are attempting to communicate with, or why bother?

When we fail to listen, we are already placed in an overly emotional state, because talking for you never stops. You are constantly engaged in conversation either with the other person or even worse in your own head. This greatly distorts communication. Our brains become over stimulated and we can't stop talking long enough to listen, long enough to process the value of what's being said (content or context) by the other person. Instead, all that is left for us to do is argue, defend, scream, curse, shut down, accuse, criticize, and interrogate.

Such habitual tactics are engaged to bring the focus back to me (I'm waving in my head). Look at me! Hear me! The operative word here is *tactic*s. As your emotions force their way front and center. Arguing, cursing, blaming, interrogating are learned behaviors for regaining all of the attention. And a gross misuse and manipulation of the phrase "whatever gets results gets repeated." If poor behavior has ever worked before, we will repeat it over and over again, even if it cost us a severed relationship. After all, if I am displaying the behaviors listed above (arguing, cursing, blaming, interrogating …), you definitely don't want the spotlight on you, do you?

This is one of those situations where power is at issue, but not the type of power you would think. I have learned that people who behave the worst, often feel the most powerless. Your beliefs, self-image and low emotional control are the internal mechanisms which fuel these abrasive actions. The yeller feels powerless and small; they want results the only way they think they can get them. While the receiver of this poor behavior simply sees this person as a controlling bully; a jerk!

This distorted perspective keeps us from reaching people, and it's also what keeps people from reaching us. This behavior fractures relationships. Both parties just want to be heard; heard beyond the words and feelings. Although, their beliefs and values, are at the heart of this dissension; too often we simply aren't able to formulate the words to adequately convey the pain we really feel. Instead all we seem to convey is "hear me" at all cost.

Of course, we all use inappropriate words at times, when we simply don't know what else to say. But to truly listen moves us beyond mere words. Listening allows you to take a holistic communication approach to the person and what's being said, that really isn't being said. If you can stop the internal and external chatter, you'll be amazed at what you hear.

One of my dear friends (Jacqueline) once shared with me a saying of her father's *"Don't drown in a cup of water!"* This is as impactful now, as it was when I first heard it. Have you ever seen a person flail around in water only waist deep; while offering the simple instructions to "Just, stand up!" Well, I'm throwing out a verbal lifeline here.... clear your mind, and listen more than you speak!

If you want to walk on water you gotta' get out of the boat.

John Ortberg

Making the communication shift:

- Listening conveys a message of value.

- Listen beyond words to the beliefs and values of the person speaking. This is at the heart of their message.

- An empty can makes the loudest noise. Yelling is not always about force, but feeling powerless, exhausted, and feeling like you're all out of options.

- Gain emotional mastery, what does this mean? Don't allow someone to pull you into an emotional cycle that defeats your intended goal. Remain calm, and remain objective, and don't be afraid to table for later what can't be resolved at the time.

CHAPTER 6
Just Ask!

YOU DESIRE BUT DO NOT HAVE, so you kill. You covet but you cannot get what you want, so you quarrel and fight... When you ask, you do not receive, because you ask with wrong motives, that you may spend what you get on your pleasures. (James 4:2-3, NIV).

We accept that communication encompasses many things; tone, inflection, gestures, adapters, reflectors and so much more. But there is a right way and a wrong way to *ask* to get what you desire. The Creator has provided explicit instructions on how we should approach Him when asking for the desires of our heart. However, we can also gain great insight into the art of asking and receiving in our personal and professional relationships from the passage written above.

Communication Strategy# 6: **Ask Like You Mean It.** According to my mother "you can say anything you want, as long as you know how to say it." I say, "You can say *almost* anything you want, if you say it, or ask it, pleasantly, positively, with respect and kindness **and the belief that you will receive it."** My version is a little lengthier I know, but it works for me.

Although, you may not have had a similar experience you were still taught the principle of asking, whether by direct instruction, example, or the lack thereof. Again, communication is passed down from generation to generation, it is imperative that we pass down the skill of *"how to ask"* down to the next generation. To genuinely consider others when requesting things of them we are intentionally passing down a skill capable of enhancing both our children's future personal and professional relationships.

So, professionally, if everything we request comes by force, simply because we are in authority, those we ask will in turn imitate and request of others also by force, or even worse, through internal retreat, by abandoning the request all together. It would be of great benefit if we concentrate our attention on relationship building, developing trust on the one hand, and seeking to understand, on the other. If we fail to do this, we create a vicious cycle of combative responses, defensiveness, distrust, avoidance, and detachment. It is the approach to asking, that moves people to meet our request.

This approach does not mean a display of weakness, by coddling, hand holding, or the use of syrupy passive language, but respect. Can you recall a time when someone spoke to you who was in authority, yet conveyed it in kindness and respect for you as a human being? It is this style of communicating whose purpose is grounded in a positive outcome. Not just in having the request fulfilled, but acknowledging the relationship which is strengthened by the request.

Constructive and compassionate language can move people in useful directions, while brutal, abusive, authoritative language can result in quarrels, fighting, bruised feelings and discord, damage, disloyalty, fear and mistrust. When we ask amiss, not believing, or ask with impure motives, for self-serving gain, or simply because you are the person with the title, it can result in verbal distortion, and the erection of walls, which may take years to break through.

It is these same walls that currently stand between many personal and professional relationships today. Unfortunately, instead of us aiding in a breakthrough, we are hurling bricks hand over fist. Again, asking is not about begging, pleading or groveling, but moving those asked to a state of completion, with a mutual benefit. There are several things to consider when asking something of someone.

1. *Don't ask amiss.* Don't ask as though you are already defeated in the request. The surest way to ensure failure is to convey uncertainty. Know what you want and be specific with your request. *Don't assume the details are obvious to everyone involved.* Move the

request visually from your head to mine. Know what you need, why you need it, and when you need it. *Describe* on paper (or in your head in a pinch) what you want, before you involve someone else. Begin by asking yourself some vital questions, when, where, how, and with whom?

2. *Ask with pure motives.* Don't have ulterior motives or hidden agendas which are only self-serving. If your request is objective based, will it help to develop trust or even some type of gain for the person performing the task? Gain doesn't always have to be tangible; money. Creating a feeling or a dream is often equally effective. Will it enhance the relationship or their career? What goals will it help to reach, personal or professional? Is there a hidden agenda that if known would create feelings of betrayal should the whole story be revealed?

3. *Ask without demeaning.* You desire but do not have, so you kill. If you have ever asked something of someone before and you feel you aren't getting the results you *think* you *deserve*, mental execution can begin. Why? If you take their denial or failure to comply as a personal attack you will feel forced to defend your position. So, you quarrel and

fight and war against yourself trying to move people to a place of submission.

You berate and create verbal conflict, because compliance becomes the only goal. Here, is a prime place to ask that you review those barriers listed in Chapter 1; these could be at the heart of an unfulfilled request. Whatever the reason, I beg of you, not to take it personal. If you do, you'll be picking up bricks before you know it and throwing them with a feverish pitch. Even if your request is fulfilled, the results may fail miserably. The deed may be done, but not to your satisfaction, and the emotional damage may linger.

Barking out orders is not the sign of a leader; instead, it's the sign of internal frustration, of someone who holds a title, without real influence. Remember, if your request goes against the beliefs and values of the person you are requesting something of, there is bound to be some level of resistance. As the requester, it is your responsibility to move me from resistance to compliance; with the utmost respect, still intact.

The closer you are to gaining a full understanding of the other person's internal experience, the more you can effect change and gain the intended outcome. This isn't snooping and having coffee at Starbucks. It's back to empathetic listening to what they aren't saying. The use of vague phrases and generalizations puts us back into that dreaded state of ambiguity, and we now know how our brains hate that.

Making assumptions is the true sign of an unskilled communicator. This is worth repeating, assumptions are the true sign of an unskilled communicator. It's also one of the most dangerous and ineffective approaches to communication there is. If we can find out what people want or need, it is easier for them and us to communicate effectively. Being attuned to beliefs and values as they surface, and knowing how to ask the right questions will take us deeper into the relationship for which we are being gifted.

Words can be walls, but they can also be bridges. It's important to use words to link people rather than divide them.

Tony Robbins

Making the communication shift:

- Ask with mutual respect.
- Don't destroy and kill inner emotions because your request isn't being fulfilled.
- Move the asked to a state of completion with clarity and pure motives.
- Consider what the barriers could be to the request.
- Choose not to take noncompliance as a personal dismissal.

CHAPTER 7
Closing the Communication Divide

WE ARE IN A COMMUNICATION CRISIS, my friend and media failed to inform us. Poor communication lies at the root of most of the issues that plague our society today; poor and failing relationships, irreconcilable differences resulting in divorce, verbal abuse, brutality, domestic violence, bullying, mismanaged leadership, lost careers, low employee morale, poorly attended social programs, and yes, even your very own negative self-talk, all have roots that emanate from the source of poor communication ability.

***Communication Strategy # 7*: Keep Calm and Prepare to**

Change.   The ability to transmit information, thoughts, ideas and

emotions, begs that we move to a more advanced level of

communication; and without an intentional communication strategy to do

so, we are left to rely on the faulty and misguided communication

devices we have inherited.

Yet another variable between a master communicator and an

unskilled communicator is the ability to be comfortable with and even

appreciate silence. Simply learning to value silence, in hopes that it will

generate a meaningful response…. wait for it… you will never know if

you don't allow it to happen. It's these moments of silence and lulls

which allow us to process the message received. Respect and even

cherish these moments of silence. Refrain from false interpretation that

all silence is a sign of disrespect, abandonment, displeasure, or anger.

Allow me to recall a story where silence was neither golden nor well received. I was called to the boss's office one day and raked over the coals about an email response I'd sent. It had been interpreted with an extremely exaggerated eye of criticism. I immediately tried defending myself against what I perceived to be a personal attack against my character.

To no avail, the harsh words continued to cut like a knife, moving me further and further away from my perception of who I believed myself to be. Over a brief few moments, suspended in time, it became painfully apparent that my boss could not be convinced of their error. I soon stopped defending (shut down), and then… there was just this weighty silence. My mind processing this unpleasant depiction, of the perception they held of me, had brought me to silence. I was speechless, as my boss's beliefs and values surfaced the more they spoke. This was not just how they saw me, but their perception of people in general. And, of course, I took it personal. I know I told you not to do that. But that was then and this now.

As I listened through the pain, one of the most illuminating statements came when they said with a heart-breaking response "Are you going to say something, or just sit there with that stupid look on your face?" I was mortified, livid, and greatest of all the emotions, was a great sadness. I was emotionally full, and all I could do was cry. I had reached emotional saturation. I never responded, as my thoughts were suspended in total disbelief.

My first thought was, why was I experiencing all these what seem to be personal emotions in a professional encounter? I concluded that too many ideologies had surfaced in this brief encounter, which could never be resolved without some form of intervention. This inaccurate perception would leave me wounded. I knew I could forgive, but I felt I could not forget. These emotions had been brought to bear over a misinterpreted email. I was forced to asked "What if I sent another email, which was poorly received?" Would I be willing to endure this overly critical humiliation again?

My boss had thrown their weight around for sure. Not only were they uncomfortable in what I had written, but they were uncomfortable with what I could not bring myself to say; my silence. I in turn was uncomfortable with their interpretation and distorted perception. I was uncomfortable in their unwillingness to allow me to clarify my intent. I was uncomfortable that they felt a need to hurt with their words. I was uncomfortable that "stupid" was a word of choice. And I was unwilling to accept their rude and terse delivery. For me the outcome could only be… separation. I would grieve the loss of the relationship, as well as the opportunity to fulfill my role.

Although, this was a severed professional relationship on my part, our personal relationships often follow the same beaten paths of dissension. Too often we hold that old familiar ideology of "us against them" with separation appearing to be the only option. Too often, we search our old familiar phrases, only to use the ones we feel will hurt the most. Just recently I heard something profound in passing "the strategy of separation creates enemies; it does not create a *pact*." I was forced to ask the question, what is a *pact*? It is a treaty; an agreement; an arrangement between people. So, when we intentionally separate we create the opposite of the desired effect; an agreement between people.

I have witnessed this first hand, and it could not ring truer! The only reason separation seems that it's the only option, is because *we think we're all out of options* and we've failed to maintain control. We perceive people who have different views as an enemy and not an ally…. Sometimes, we get it wrong. Sometimes, it's neither, and we are simply unaware of how to develop the latter.

With an unquenchable desire to elevate our communication ability we can begin to salvage these once meaningful relationships that appear to be coming to an abrupt end. "How, you ask?" Let me take you back to the beginning, by reiterating that communication is **everything** you do. What you are communicating is who you are, and it is not confined to what you say. If only we were more conscious of the barriers that divert and hijack our communication attempts, and seek to remove them whenever possible. If we could get out of our feelings, the resentment, animosity, visions of failure and false perceptions, and simply reason from a place of logic.

If only we could move our communication to a place that is outcome driven and not self-serving. If we could learn to minimize the ambiguity and fill in our own blanks; or isolate and destroy the negative chatter with a more positive story. If we could develop our ability to present a more congruent message; instead of saying one thing while your body language reveals something different. If only we could learn to ask with respect and humility; while boldly believing, we will receive. If we could learn to cherish the moments of silence and listen more than we speak.... What a wonderful world this would be (in my Sam Cooke voice). The barricades between people become barriers to success and happiness, so getting through it is not just a fine art—it's a crucial skill. Let us rethink, reevaluate, and in many instances reinvent, and refocus our communication efforts, because my dear reader, indeed, talk *is* cheap, until it costs you *everything!*

The Tiny Tweaks that Elevate Your Communication

- Redefine communication to encompass everything you do instead of just the method used.
- Consider the possible barriers if you're not getting through.
- Resist the need to place personal blame and keep score.
- If at first you don't succeed, try, try again and again.
- Bring your thoughts under your subjection instead of letting them run amuck and ruin your communication.
- Skewed perceptions tend to amplify or diminish data, regardless of facts.
- Don't allow poor perceptions to reign supreme.
- Take 100% responsibility and control of all of your emotions.
- If you are emotionally distressed about a situation or circumstance it is due to your own estimate of how you see it. You can change it.
- This isn't easy. Our minds resist paradigm shifts-we don't like to change our fundamental perceptions of life.
- Once you master your emotions, your life and the way you communicate will never be the same.
- Alter your expectations, if you look for good you'll find it.
- Resist being overly critical, it stunts relationship growth.
- Refrain from using words like "never" and "always" unless used in positive context.
- Listening conveys a message of value.
- Listen beyond words to the beliefs and values of the person speaking. This is at the heart of their message.

- An empty can makes the loudest noise. Yelling is not always about force, but feeling powerless, exhausted, and feeling like you're all out of options.
- Ask with mutual respect.
- Don't destroy and kill inner emotions because your request isn't being fulfilled.
- Move the person asked to a state of completion with clarity and pure motives.
- Consider what the possible barriers could be to the request.
- In all your communication exchanges, choose not to take it personal.
- Individuals communicate within their own frames of reference, understanding and perceptions and rarely is what they say or do about you specifically.

Invitation

We hope you found this information valuable, and if it resonates with you. We invite you to connect with us. I will walk you through a more in-depth overview of communication strategies while helping you develop the next level of your personal or professional communication journey.

Get all the information to join "**The Communication Revolution**" by

visiting: www.obecommunicationcoach.com

We'd love to be a part of your communication transformation.

As Your Communication Strategist I Will:

- Lift and support you through the communication obstacles you are currently facing; personal or professional.

- Engage in dialogue with you by asking, requesting and listening to what your communication needs are.

- I will empower you to implement your own strategic communication devices.

- I will aid you in seeking the answers to habits and cycles of communication that may have failed you in the past.
- Focus on the process that improves the bottom line and produces results.

- I will celebrate your learning and your growth every step of the way.

A Strategic Approach Can Make the Difference

☐   Do you seem to struggle in interviews?

☐   Do you want to request an increase in pay and aren't sure how?

☐   Are you ever frustrated in how people perceive you?

☐   Do you tend to have the same argument over and over again and feel as though you and your partner will never see eye to eye?

☐   Is your company's turnover way to frequent?

☐   Do you feel forced to leave a job or career you love?

☐   Do you jump to conclusions or ruminate over things you wish you would have said?

☐   Do your beliefs and values come across as frustration and confusion?

☐   Are your negative thoughts getting in the way of how you communicate?

I can help....

OBE's communication approach is one of perspective, value and clarity...we seek to bridge ALL conversations.

Services

☐   Workshops

☐   Seminars

☐   Private one on one coaching

☐   Public speaking engagements.

You can reach Avis P. Robinson at email:

obecommunicationcoaching@gmail.com.

Sign up for our quarterly newsletter at

www.obecommunicaioncoach.com/contact

References

Arden, J. B. (2010). *Rewire your brain*. Hoboken, NJ: John Wiley & Sons, Inc.

Covey, S. (2004). *The 7 habits of highly effective people: Powerful lessons in personal change*. New York, NY: Simon & Schuster.

Duck, S. (1994). Steady as (s) he goes: Relational maintenance as a shared meaning system. In Canary, D. J.; Stafford, L. (Eds.), *Communication and Relational maintenance* (pp.45-60). San Diego, CA: Academic Press, Inc.

Greene, R. (1998). *The 48 laws of power*. Johannesburg, South Africa: Penguin Books, Ltd.

Robbins, T. (1998). *Unlimited Power*. New York, NY: A Division of Simon & Schuster, Inc.

Tracy, B. (2012). *Earn what you are really worth*. New York, NY: Vanguard Press.

About the Author

Avis P. Robinson, is the Founder & CEO of On Bended Ear |Communication Consulting Agency. For more than 15 years, Avis has been involved in leadership and mentorship; working in the capacity as both upper and middle management. Avis holds a Master's degree in Strategic Communication, and a Bachelor's degree in Nonprofit Leadership and Management; her foresight and business acumen are vast.

She has taught hundreds of classes on effective communication, personal development and job readiness, and has both transformed and impacted countless lives along the way. Avis is both innovative and creative and has taught classes for students' ages 6-60.

She believes you're only as effective as the impact you leave on your audience, and only as good as the last class taught. Avis knows assuredly that she was born and preserved to make a difference; and what she does along the journey is simply to fulfill her life's purpose and divine assignment.

Her favorite quote "When you change the way you look at things, the things you look at change" is a testament to confirm that life is about perspective, and change is first realized internally. This approach leads to true empowerment, actualization, peace and freedom. Her passion for effective and meaningful communication surpasses mere words, and encompasses the whole being of the people she has been placed here to serve.